soho theatre

C000164378

onreligion

by Mick Gordon and A C Grayling

First performed at Soho Theatre on 28 November 2006

Cast

Grace	Gemma Jones
Tom	Elliot Levey
Tony	Pip Donaghy
Ruth	Priyanga Burford

Creative Team

Director	Mick Gordon
Designer	Naomi Wilkinson
Lighting Designer	Linus Fellbom
Sound Designer	Mike Furness
Composer	Jon Frankel
Assistant Director	Christopher Haydon
Production Manager	Nick Ferguson
Stage Manager	Sarah Buik
Deputy Stage Manager	Hannah Ashwell-Dickinson
Set built by	Robert Knight
Casting	Nadine Hoare
On Theatre Administrator	Martha O'Toole

Biographies

Priyanga Burford Ruth

After studying English at Keble College, Oxford, Priyanga trained at LAMDA. On leaving drama school she won the Carleton Hobbs award and worked with the BBC Radio Drama Company. Her theatre credits include work with the Royal Shakespeare Company, the Young Vic, the Gate, Shared Experience, and her own company InService Productions. Her work in television includes *Extras*, *Murphy's Law*, *Casualty*, *The Vice*, *Heartless* and *A Rather English Marriage*. Last year Priyanga's first short screenplay, *Graham and Alice*, was produced by the BBC.

Pip Donaghy Tony

Most recently Pip has been touring Australia playing the title role in *An Inspector Calls* and at Chichester Festival Theatre playing Wackford Squeers, Mulberry Hawk and Wagstaff in *Nicholas Nickleby*. His many roles at the National Theatre include Jesus in *The Passion*, Clytemnestra in *The Oresteia*, Napoleon Pig in *Animal Farm*, Sir Lucius O'Trigger in *The Rivals*, Sartorius in *Widowers' Houses*, Aslaksen in *An Enemy of the People*. For the RSC: Sir Harry Wildair in *The Constant Couple*, Freeman in *The Plain Dealer*, Medley in *The Man of Mode*. For Shared Experience: *Mill on the Floss*, *A Doll's House*, *The Clearing*. Pip started in Rep in 1969 and has toured extensively with 7:84, Joint Stock and English Touring Theatre. Favourite roles to date: Elliot in *Private Lives*, Captain Boyle in *Juno and the Paycock* at Manchester Exchange and Contact Theatre.

Linus Fellbom
Lighting Designer

Since his debut as a lighting designer in 1995, Linus has designed over 100 productions. He has worked at most of the bigger venues around Sweden and has also been engaged at theatres and opera houses in cities such as Oldenburg, Berlin, Innsbruck, Riga, Lodz, Warsaw, Cape Town, London, Oslo and Copenhagen. In October 2005 Linus made his debut as a stage director with *Sympathy for the Devil* by Lucas Svensson at Strindberg's Intimate Theatre in Stockholm. In October 2006 he directed William Shakespeare's *Richard III* for Riksteatern in Sweden.

Jon Frankel Composer

Music for theatre includes *A Prayer for Owen Meany* (National Theatre), *Salome* (National Theatre Studio), *Measure for Measure* (English Touring Theatre), *The Promise* (Battersea Arts Centre) and *Alice in Wonderland* (Royal Parks).

Mike Furness Sound Designer

Theatre sound designs include: *All's Well That Ends Well* and *As You Like It* (RSC); *Blues In The Night*, *The Witches*, *Ladyday*, *The BFG* (West End); *Mother Courage* (National Theatre) and shows for The Tricycle, Paines Plough, Theatre Royal Stratford East, Lyric Hammersmith, Birmingham Rep, West Yorkshire Playhouse, Bristol Old Vic, Brighton and Edinburgh Festivals. In 2006: *A Fine Balance* (Hampstead Theatre), *Babe* (Regents Park), *The Trouble With Asian Men* (Soho Theatre). He also produces Talking Books and designs sound for a diverse range of live events.

Mick Gordon Writer / Director

For On Theatre: *On Ego*, Soho Theatre, London; *On Love in Uzbekistan,* Ilhom Theatre, Tashkent; *On Love, On Death,* Gate Theatre, London. Other theatre includes: *Optic Trilogy, A Play in Swedish, English and Italian,* Dramatan Theatre, Stockholm; *War, Lovers, The Real Thing, Betrayal,* Strindberg Theatre, Stockholm, Critics Award Best Production; *A Prayer for Owen Meany, The Walls, Le Pub!,* National Theatre, London; *Monkey!,* Young Vic Theatre, London; *Trust,* Royal Court Theatre; *Salome,* Riverside Studios; *Godspell,* Chichester Festival Theatre; *My Fair Lady, Closer, Art,* National Theatre Buenos Aires, ACE Award Best Production; *Volunteers, Marathon, Une Tempete,* Gate Theatre, London; *Measure for Measure,* English Touring Theatre; *The Promise, Arabian Nights,* BAC.

A C Grayling Writer

A C Grayling MA, DPhil (Oxon) FRSA is Professor of Philosophy at Birkbeck College, University of London, and a Supernumerary Fellow of St Anne's College, Oxford. He has written and edited many books on philosophy and other subjects, for several years wrote the *Last Word* column for the *Guardian*, and is a regular reviewer for the *Literary Review, Independent on Sunday, Financial Times,* and other newspapers and magazines. A frequent broadcaster on BBC Radios 4, 3 and the World Service, and a regular panelist on BBC 4's *The World*, he is the Editor of *Online Review London*, and Contributing Editor of *Prospect* magazine. In 2003 he was a Booker Prize judge.

Christopher Haydon
Assistant Director

Studied Theology at Cambridge University and trained at Central. Directing credits include: *Notes from Underground* (Arcola Theatre); *Come and Go, Agamemnon* (Embassy Studio); *The Maids* (Embassy Theatre) and *The Insect Play* (Emmanuel College, Cambridge). As assistant director: *The Desire Tree* (a Zygo Arts co-production with the Oxford Playhouse/Tumanishvili Theatre, Tbilisi, Georgia); *The Found Man* (Traverse Theatre, Edinburgh). He was assistant producer on *Remembering Buzz*, an event held by the RSC. He has written for *The Scotsman* and the *Financial Times*.

Gemma Jones Grace

Gemma Jones trained at RADA, where she won the Gold Medal in 1962. Among her many theatrical credits are *Hamlet* at the Birmingham Rep, Peter Brook's *A Midsummer Night's Dream* RSC world tour, *A Streetcar Named Desire* at the Nottingham Playhouse, *Cabaret* at the Sheffield Crucible and *Cat On a Hot Tin Roof* at the Lyric Theatre. On television she has appeared in, among other things, *The Spoils of Poynton, The Seagull, The Cherry Orchard* and *Jane Eyre*. She played the eponymous heroine Louisa Trotter in the BBC series *The Duchess of Duke Street* and, on film, Emma Thompson's mother in Ang Lee's *Sense and Sensibility*. She plays Madam Pomfrey in *Harry Potter* and Bridget's mother in *Bridget Jones' Diary*.

Elliot Levey Tom

Elliot Levey's work in theatre includes *On Ego* and *On Love* for On Theatre, *Henry IV parts One and Two* and *His Dark Materials* (National Theatre); *Beasts & Beauties* (Bristol Old Vic); *Tonight We Fly* (Trestle Theatre); *Monkey!* (Young Vic); *The Comedy Of Errors* (RSC and Young Vic); *Love's Work* (Gate) and *Perdition* (Gate, as director); *Proposals* (West Yorkshire Playhouse); *The Tempest* (British Council World Tour); *The Reckless are Dying Out* (Lyric Hammersmith); *Macbeth* (Piccadilly); *Cyrano de Bergerac* (The Bridewell); *Tonguetied* (Young Vic Studio); *The Warp at Three Mills Island*, *Passion*, *If I Were Lifted Up from Earth*, *Milk and Blood* and *Arabian Nights* (Battersea Arts Centre); *The Soldier's Tale* at Theatre Artaud; *Le Pub!*, *Tales of Hoffman*, *Charlie and the Chocolate Factory*, *The Prince* (NT studio). Television includes *EastEnders, Holby City, Beau Brummell, Casualty 1906, Amnesia, Doctors, Sirens, Empire, A Lump in My Throat, Fat Friends, Lovejoy*. Film includes *The Queen, Song of Songs, The Gospel of John, Supertex, An Hour in Paradise, Judas, Jason and the Argonauts, The Low Down, Jesus, Before the Law, Wildwood*. Radio includes *The Radetsky March* and *Love's Work*.

Martha O'Toole Administrator

Previous to joining On Theatre for last year's *On Ego*, Martha worked in Chicago with Lookingglass Theatre, Redmoon Theatre, A Red Orchid Theatre and Theatre Oobleck and with Holland's Dogtroep (for the Chicago International Theatre Festival).

Naomi Wilkinson Designer

Recent credits include: *A Midsummer Night's Dream* (Dundee Rep) *Just for Show* (National Theatre, with Lloyd Newson, DV8 Physical Theatre), *The Misanthrope* (Guildhall School of Music & Drama), *Accidental Death of an Anarchist* (Octagon Theatre), *Don't Look Back* (Dreamthinkspeak / a site-specific piece at The General Register House in Edinburgh, Total Theatre Award 2005, Edinburgh Festival), *The Firework Maker's Daughter* (Sheffield Crucible & Lyric Theatre Hammersmith), *I'm a Fool to Want You* (BAC/ Tron Theatre). Other credits include: *4.48 Psychosis* (Directed by Kathryn Hunter, LAMDA), *Colder Than Here* (Soho Theatre), *Happy Yet?* (Gate Theatre), *Arcane* (Opera Circus, Lilian Baylis Theatre & UK Tour), *Don't Look Back* (Dreamthinkspeak Stanmer House, Brighton Festival/ State Cinema Grays/ South Hill Park, Bracknell & Somerset House London), *I Weep at my Piano* (BAC), *Wrong Place* (Soho Theatre), *Happy Birthday Mr Deka D* (Traverse Theatre), *Shoot Me in the Heart* (Gate Theatre), *Aladdin* (Lyric Theatre Hammersmith), *A little Fantasy* (Soho Theatre), *I Can't Wake Up* (Lyric Theatre Studio), *Gobbledygook* (Gogmagogs, Traverse Theatre), *Mules* (Clean Break, Royal Court Theatre upstairs), *Two Horsemen* (Gate Theatre), *My Life in the Bush of Ghosts* and *Heredity* (both Royal Court Theatre Upstairs).

Thanks

Many people have contributed to the making of **On Religion**.
Thanks to:

Tariq Ramadan
Dr Azzam Tamimi
Dr Fraser Watts
Prof Alister McGrath
Dr Abdelwahab El-Affendi
Nawaal Deane
Yumnah Du Toit
Tanya Ritchie
Prof Richard Dawkins
Dr Michael Persinger
Archbishop Rowan Williams
Prof John Gray
Don Cupitt
Baroness Julia Neuberger
Rabbi Tony Hammond
Prof Lewis Wolpert
Matthew Wolpert
Muhammad Yusuf Al-Husseini
Dr Gervase Rosser
Dr Jane Garnett
Danny Friedman
Gavin Irwin
Faber and Faber
art meets matter
Orion Books
And as ever, Nici Butchart

Thanks also to Adam Glass
and the Board of On Theatre

Joe Smith

The team at Soho Theatre

Lisa Goldman

Mark Godfrey

Especially Nina Steiger

The editors at Oberon
Books Dan Steward and Will
Hammond

Sian Alexander

Jef Higgins

Thanks to Sian Ede and
the Calouste Gulbenkian
Foundation who supported the
development process

Thanks to publishers James
Hogan and Charles Glanville
for their generous support

Iona Firouzabadi

Elisabeth Morse

**And a very special thanks to
Rev Giles Fraser**

A C Grayling would like to thank the National Secular Society and
the British Humanist Association.

Naomi Wilkinson would like to thank Charles Mason.

On Religion is supported by New Humanist magazine.

On Theatre is supported by  CALOUSTE
GULBENKIAN
FOUNDATION

● soho theatre

- produces new work
- discovers and nurtures new writers
- targets and develops new audiences

Soho Theatre Company is passionate in its commitment to new writing, producing a year-round programme of bold, original and accessible new plays – many of them from first-time playwrights.

> *'a foundry for new talent... one of the country's leading producers of new writing'* Evening Standard

Soho Theatre offers an invaluable resource to emerging playwrights. Our training and outreach programme includes the innovative Under 11s scheme, the Young Writers' Group (15-25s) and a burgeoning series of writing workshops designed to equip new writers with the basic tools of playwriting. We offer the nation's only unsolicited script-reading service, reporting on over 2,000 plays per year. We aim to develop and showcase the most promising new work through the national Verity Bargate Award, the Launch Pad scheme and the Writers' Attachment Programme, working to develop writers not just in theatre but also for TV and film.

> *'a creative hotbed... not only the making of theatre but the cradle for new screenplay and television scripts'* The Times

Contemporary, comfortable, air-conditioned and accessible, Soho Theatre is busy from early morning to late at night. Alongside the production of new plays, it is also an intimate venue to see leading national and international comedians in an eclectic programme mixing emerging new talent with established names.

> *'London's coolest theatre by a mile'* Midweek

● soho theatre

Soho Theatre, 21 Dean St, London W1D 3NE; Admin: 020 7287 5060; Box Office: 0870 429 6883; www.sohotheatre.com

The Terrace Bar
The Terrace Bar on the second floor serves a range of soft and alcoholic drinks.

Email information list
For regular programme updates and offers visit www.sohotheatre.com

Hiring the theatre
Soho Theatre has a range of rooms and spaces for hire. Please contact the theatre managers on 020 7287 5060 or go to www.sohotheatre.com for further details.

SUPPORTING SOHO THEATRE

Soho Theatre receives core funding from Arts Council England, London. In order to provide as diverse a programme as possible, to expand our audience development and to extend our outreach work, we rely increasingly upon additional support from trusts, foundations, individuals and businesses.

All of our major sponsors share a common commitment to developing new areas of activity and encouraging creative partnerships between business and the arts. We tailor sponsorship opportunities to accommodate all needs, and also have a Business membership scheme offering a wide range benefits.

We are immensely grateful for the invaluable support from our sponsors and donors and wish to thank them for their continued commitment.

STAFF
Artistic Director: Lisa Goldman
Executive Director: Mark Godfrey

Board of Directors
Nicholas Allott - chair
Sue Robertson - vice chair
Sophie Clarke-Jervoise
Norma Heyman
Roger Jospé
Michael Naughton
David Pelham
Dr Simon Singh MBE
Roger Wingate
Christopher Yu

Honorary Patrons
Bob Hoskins - president
Peter Brook CBE
Simon Callow
Sir Richard Eyre CBE

Mick Gordon and A C Grayling

ON RELIGION

A Theatre Essay

OBERON BOOKS
LONDON

First published in 2006 by Oberon Books Ltd
521 Caledonian Road, London N7 9RH
Tel: 020 7607 3637 / Fax: 020 7607 3629
e-mail: info@oberonbooks.com
www.oberonbooks.com

A catalogue record for this book is available from the British
Library.

Cover image: Getty Images / Cover design by Jane Harper

ISBN: 1 84002 714 2 / 978-1-84002-714-3

Printed in Great Britain by Antony Rowe Ltd, Chippenham

theatre *n.* 1 A building designed for the performance of plays, operas, etc. 2 The writing or production of plays. 3 A setting for dramatic or important events. [From Latin *theatrum,* from Greek *theatron,* place for viewing.]

essay *n.* 1 A short literary composition dealing with a subject analytically or speculatively. 2 To attempt or endeavour; effort. 3 To test or try out. [From Old French *essaier,* to attempt.]

Characters

GRACE
A Professor of Natural Science. In her sixties.

TOM
Grace's son. Early thirties.

TONY
Grace's husband. A retired English teacher

RUTH
Tom's girlfriend. Early 30s.

DR MICHAEL PERSINGER
is voiced by the actor playing Tony

Scene 1

GRACE is sitting in Dr Michael Persinger's Transcranial Magnetic Stimulator. She sits with ping-pong ball halves taped over her eyes and wearing a yellow motorcycle helmet that has been fitted with electrodes, aimed at her temples. She looks and feels like a surreally enthroned Pope.

GRACE: Hello?

> Anybody out there?

> *Waits. No Answer.*

> Clearly not.

> *A crackle of an old loud speaker.*

> Michael?

> *Another crackle. Then the disembodied voice of the American scientist MICHAEL PERSINGER.*

MICHAEL: Yes. Sorry. Hello?

GRACE: I'm not sure this is working. Nothing seems to be happening.

> *GRACE makes to remove the apparatus.*

MICHAEL: *No!* Don't touch that! Sorry Professor, no, you're right, nothing is happening.

GRACE: I can feel a sort of buzzing, slightly, but that's all. Although that could be my ears. They buzz sometimes when I'm nervous.

MICHAEL: We're just checking the system. A connection must be loose.

GRACE: If I had known that having a religious experience was going to be as complicated as this I might actually have considered going to church.

MICHAEL laughs.

Buzzing's stopped.

MICHAEL: Great. That must have been it. How you doing in there?

GRACE: Fine.

MICHAEL: I always get a little claustrophobic myself.

GRACE: Sorry?

MICHAEL: When I'm in the chair.

GRACE: Oh right.

MICHAEL: Under the Helmet. One time I even thought the room was hexed!

GRACE: Hexed?

MICHAEL: Can you believe that?

GRACE: I'm not sure. Depends on what hexed means exactly.

MICHAEL: It's slang, you know, for what witches do. Spells! No, jinxes! Do you say jinx in England?

GRACE: We can.

MICHAEL: Well, it's the same as jinxed. I thought the room was jinxed!

GRACE: Gosh.

MICHAEL: And that was before they switched on the electro-magnets! (*Chuckles.*) But don't worry. If you do find yourself becoming frightened or perturbed even just speak up and we'll stop.

GRACE: Good.

MICHAEL: If you think you *see* something for example...

GRACE: Right.

MICHAEL: Or sense a *presence…*

GRACE: Okay.

MICHAEL: Something that makes you feel *uncomfortable…*

GRACE: Yes.

MICHAEL: You just have to say the word…

GRACE: I get it Michael, lest you be accused of leading the witness.

MICHAEL: Excuse me? Ah yes. Ha! Right. Okay, we're almost set. Shall I walk you through the process?

GRACE: Please.

MICHAEL: Well as you know, all perception and thought is based on electrical activity in the brain. And what I'm attempting to do is identify the specific electric pulses that cause specific brain reactions. One induces the mystical feelings we're trying for today, another a general feeling of well-being, another creates sexual arousal.

GRACE: I should have brought Tony.

MICHAEL: Who's Tony?

GRACE: My husband. Sorry. Sort of a joke reflex. I can never resist.

MICHAEL: Unlike Tony.

GRACE: Excuse me?

MICHAEL: Unlike Tony. He can resist.

GRACE: Yes, quite, very good.

MICHAEL: (*Chuckling.*) You should have brought Tony. Funny.

GRACE: So God is an energy field.

MICHAEL: The electrics of the brain. Now the Helmet itself isn't dangerous. The magnetic field it produces is no stronger than the field produced by an average hair dryer.

GRACE: An average hair dryer?

MICHAEL: No more than that.

GRACE: Does that not beg a serious question?

MICHAEL: Many questions Professor. Many questions. Okay. We're good to go. You ready Professor?

GRACE: As I'll ever be.

MICHAEL: Then I'll see you on the other side.

Moves fluidly into:

Scene 2

The evening before TOM's summing up speech, he is ironing tomorrow's shirt while rehearsing in front of RUTH. She is wearing pyjamas and eating take-away food

TOM: Ladies and Gentlemen I don't need to tell you how serious this allegation is, I don't need to tell you how serious the implications are for my client, for my client's family, and for his community if you convict him. I don't need to tell you… The judge is going to butt in.

RUTH: Not if you sell it.

TOM: (*Shaking his head.*) I don't need to tell you that political decisions will probably be made as a result of your verdict. That there is a jury of public opinion watching you the jury of law. But today not I…

RUTH: Come on Tom stop being crap, put some passion into it.

TOM: I hate this.

RUTH: Pretend you're thingy in you know.

TOM: What?

RUTH: That film.

TOM: The guy's guilty as hell.

RUTH: Minorities need defending.

TOM: But why do I have to do it?!

RUTH: Because you chose to.

TOM: Did I?

RUTH: If we're not standing by the most vulnerable then why are we lawyers?

TOM: To get to the truth!

RUTH: Tom Cruise!

TOM: Tom Cruise? (*Correcting her.*) Jack Nicholson!

RUTH: No, Jack Nicholson's the other one.

TOM: You can't handle the truth!

RUTH: Truth's an ironic concept in a criminal trial.

TOM: How can you say that?

RUTH: Because it's about *proof* not truth.

TOM: And that's why I hate it.

RUTH: But today not I…

TOM: But today not I, not the Prosecution Counsel, not the J…

RUTH: Not *even.*

TOM: Not even the Judge can tell you what to do. Today ladies and gentlemen of the jury you are sovereign. A sovereign parliament of twelve and you the parliament must not convict my client unless you are sure beyond all reasonable doubt of his guilt. Now what does that mean

    – Reasonable Doubt? What does it mean? Absolutely
nothing!

RUTH: Tom!

TOM: Did you know that modern Arabic has no word for
Israeli so when they refer to Israelis they have to say Jews?

RUTH: Fifty years Tom. Fifty years! That bloke who sent his
girlfriend on the El Al plane got forty-three, and the bomb
didn't even go off.

TOM: She was pregnant.

RUTH: What?

TOM: The girlfriend on the plane. She was pregnant.

RUTH: Fifty years. He'll be seventy. He's just a boy.

    Beat.

TOM: Reasonable doubt is the central organising principle
of criminal law in this country and it insists that the
prosecution needs to supply you the jury with such proof,
proof of such a convincing character, that you would be
willing to rely and act upon it – without hesitation – in the
most important of your own affairs. This is…reasonable
doubt… Reasonable… I can't.

RUTH: Ahhh!!

TOM: (*Suddenly animated.*) Would you be able to say beyond
reasonable doubt what you ate for lunch two weeks ago,
the Tuesday before last say? I couldn't. Honestly I couldn't.
Can you even say beyond reasonable doubt that your
birthday is your birthday? I can't. In this country you used
to have up to six weeks to go and register a birth. So up to
six weeks after the most jubilant and traumatic event in an
adult life your birth was registered by one of your parents.
Now just look at my parents – how reasonable are they?

RUTH: You can't use the phrase directly.

TOM: What?

RUTH: Reasonable doubt, you mustn't say it, you'll sound like an idiot. (*Improvised and brilliant.*) Members of the jury, you have taken an oath to try this case on the evidence. And the prosecution must prove their case on the evidence presented to you in this court. Not on conjecture or surmise. Not on some vague notion of guilt by association. Not on difference. Not on common sense expressions like there's no smoke without fire. And not on the fear, the fear that we, all of us, sometimes feel in these extraordinary times. And the prosecution must prove their case to an incredibly high standard. They must make you, members of the jury *sure*. What does that mean? How are we to know what *sure* means? Well it means that if you think the defendant may be guilty then it is your duty to acquit him. Your duty. Your duty sworn on an oath.

Moves fluidly into:

Scene 3

GRACE's helmet experience. She imagines a domestic scene where her family set the breakfast table.

GRACE: And different subjects tend to label this ghostly perception with the names that their cultures have taught them: Elijah, Jesus, the Virgin Mary, Mohammed, the Sky Spirit.

TONY: The Sky Spirit?

RUTH: Native Americans…presumably.

GRACE: Right.

TONY: Gosh.

TOM: And who did you, y'know, did you see anyone?

GRACE: You don't *see* exactly.

TOM: No?

GRACE: No. They put ping-pong balls over your eyes and get you to stare at a red light.

TONY: Ping-pong balls?

GRACE: Yes. They're to reduce extraneous stimulation. They help the subject to concentrate.

TONY: To concentrate?

GRACE: Yes. Then he talks you through the process, but you don't…

TONY: So how can you see the red light?

GRACE: What?

TONY: You said you had to stare at a red light.

GRACE: Yes.

TONY: But if they put ping-pong balls over your eyes how can you see it?

GRACE: I don't know Tony you just can. It must glow through the plastic or something.

TONY: I'm only asking.

RUTH: Where shall I put these?

TONY: I'll do it.

TOM: How do they give it to you? The religious experience?

GRACE: You have to wear a sort of motorcycle helmet…

TONY: Motorcycle helmet?

GRACE: Which holds the electrodes in the correct position.

TONY: Electrodes?

GRACE: They call it the God Helmet.

TONY: The God Helmet?

GRACE: Yes and will you please stop repeating everything I say. It makes it all sound ridiculous.

TONY: Does it? Sorry.

GRACE: Anyway, you were the one who told me to go.

TONY: Right.

GRACE: You don't *see* anything, it's more like feeling something, a presence.

TOM: Like a ghost?

GRACE: Some people do describe it like feeling the presence of a ghost. Basically what they're trying to do is to stimulate the right hemisphere of the brain in the region they best think controls ideas of self and then stimulate the left hemisphere, the language centre, which interprets the stimulation as a sort of sensed entity.

TONY: And this man actually get paid to do this?

GRACE: It's important work…

TONY: Right.

GRACE: Michael Persinger thinks it's this stimulation and misinterpretation that's responsible for almost anything we describe as paranormal: aliens, heavenly apparitions, dead relatives. The implications are huge.

TOM: 'I see dead people.'

RUTH: What's that from?

TOM: That film with thingy in it.

TONY: Well I for one prefer life to have a little more mystery. And I refuse to let anyone reduce my sense of the spiritual to brain static. Especially a Canadian.

GRACE: He's not a Canadian, he's an American.

TONY: Well what's he doing in Canada then?

GRACE: It's just where he works.

TONY: Come off it. No one just works in Canada. It all sounds highly suspicious if you ask me.

GRACE: Well no one did dear.

TONY: The God Helmet.

TOM: So who did you see?

TONY: Talk about leading the witness.

GRACE: Sorry?

TOM: So who did you see?

RUTH: Sense. *The Sixth Sense*!

TOM: *The Sixth Sense.*

RUTH: Bruce Willis!

TOM: Bruce Willis! So who did you sense mum? Who did you sense?

Beat.

GRACE: (*To her son.*) You.

A moment between GRACE and TOM. TOM exits.

TONY: So who did you sense Grace? Did you sense anyone?

GRACE: No. I… No. It didn't really work on me. I just sort of felt floaty and remembered the time you went down on me in the rowing boat.

RUTH: (*A little shriek of joy.*) Ah!

GRACE: What?

RUTH: In a rowing boat?

GRACE: Yes.

RUTH: In a rowing boat?!

GRACE: Yes!

TONY: Grace!

RUTH: And Tony?

TONY: What?

RUTH: In a rowing boat!

TONY: No.

GRACE: Oh stop being so coy. Yes, a rowing boat.

RUTH: That is…!

TONY: Coy? I'm not being coy.

GRACE: It's fine when you're the one doing the talking but as soon as someone else…

RUTH: (*Delighted.*) Okay stop. This is getting disgusting.

GRACE: No it wasn't actually. I seem to remember it was totally fabulous.

TONY: I am not being coy. It's just that I've never been with you in a rowing boat.

GRACE: You bloody well have.

TONY: Honestly Grace, I haven't.

GRACE: You liar.

TONY: Never.

Beat. Then GRACE suddenly remembers.

GRACE: Oh my God.

Moves fluidly into:

Scene 4

Before. GRACE is giving a lecture. She wears a gown. We can hear sounds of a lecture theatre and on a screen see a close-up of an eye which appears as a still photograph but which will slowly close at the end of the lecture

GRACE: The classic historical example for intelligent design comes from the eighteenth-century British theologian-naturalist, William Paley, and it's known as the Watchmaker argument. Paley put it like this:

Imagine you are crossing a heath, when you strike your foot against a small object. You reach down to see what it is and find yourself picking up a stone. Looking at it you begin to wonder how the stone came to be there. And you come to the conclusion, that, for all you know, the stone has been there for ever.

Now suppose that when you had reached down you hadn't found a stone beside your shoe but a watch. You pick it up, and looking at it you begin to wonder how the watch came to be there.

Now, says William Paley, you're hardly going to think of the answer which you had given before, that for as much as you knew, the watch might have always been there. Not at all. What you're going to think is: This watch can't always have been here because this watch must have had a maker: There must have existed, at some time, and at some place or other, a designer of this watch, who formed it for the purpose which we find it actually to answer; who comprehended its construction, and designed its use.

Every indication of contrivance, insists Paley, every manifestation of design, which exists in the watch, exists in the stone. There's no difference, he says, except that in works of nature the degree of design is so sophisticated as to exceed all computation. His conclusion is simple: The marks of design in nature are too strong to be ignored. And design must have a designer. And that designer, he insists, is GOD.

Now William Paley makes his argument with passionate sincerity and it is informed by the best biological scholarship of the eighteenth century. But it is bollocks. Complete and utter bollocks. The analogy between telescope and eye, between watch and living organism, is a false one. The only watchmaker in nature is the blind force of physics. A true watchmaker has foresight: he designs his cogs and springs, and plans their interconnections with a future purpose in his mind's eye. Natural selection, the blind unconscious, automatic process which Charles Darwin discovered, and which we now know is the explanation for the existence and apparently purposeful form of all life, has no purpose in mind. In fact it is purpose-less. It does not plan for the future. It has no vision, no foresight, no sight at all. If natural selection can be said to play the role of watchmaker in nature, it is, the blind watchmaker.

Moves fluidly into:

Scene 5

After TOM's trial. GRACE is sitting on her garden swing being gently pushed by RUTH. TOM is reading from 'Alice Through the Looking Glass'. Beside him, a small pile of books, including a Bible and the complete works of Philip Larkin.

TOM: '…and at the thought of her loneliness two large tears came rolling down her cheeks. "Oh, don't go on like that!" cried the poor Queen, wringing her hands in despair. "Consider what a great girl you are. Consider what a long way you've come today. Consider what o'clock it is. Consider anything, only don't cry!" Alice could not help laughing at this even in the midst of her tears. "Can you keep from crying by considering things?" she asked.

"That's the way it's done," the Queen said with great decision: "nobody can do two things at once you know. Let's consider your age to begin with – how old are you?"'

GRACE: Seven.

TOM: "'Seven and a half exactly.'"

RUTH: I was seventeen.

TOM: "'You needn't say exactly," the Queen remarked, "I can believe it without that. Now I'll give you something to believe. I'm just one hundred and one, five months and a day."'

RUTH: Tom stop it.

GRACE: Where's Mummy now? With the angels. Living with God.

TOM: "'I can't believe that!" said Alice. "Can't you?" the Queen said in a pitying tone. "Try again, draw a long breath, and shut your eyes." Alice laughed. "There's no use trying," she said. "One can't believe impossible things."'

GRACE: I knew he was making it up. Trying to help. Trying to make me feel better.

TOM: "'I daresay you haven't had much practice," said the Queen. "When I was your age, I always did it for half an hour a day. Why, sometimes I've believed as many as six impossible things before breakfast."'

GRACE: But why didn't she want to stay at home with us? Didn't she love us enough? What did you do wrong? What did I do wrong? She did love us, you did nothing wrong, it's just that we don't decide when it's our time to go, God does. And some people who are very, very special – this was the worst part, when I knew it was definitely a lie, the part I couldn't forgive him for – some *special* people are chosen by God to go and be with Him early. And Mummy was very special. Wasn't she? I mean what was I going to say to that?

RUTH: Yes.

GRACE: What a terrible thing to do to a child.

TOM: Grandpa was old school. A real traditionalist. He hadn't a clue how to talk to children.

RUTH: I was ten years older and had the same questions.

GRACE: I think you may have had more to deal with than I did.

RUTH: Really?

GRACE: From what I gather.

RUTH: Oh?

GRACE: From Tom. He told me about your Mother…

RUTH: Oh.

GRACE: And how you were the one who found her…

TOM: Mum.

RUTH: Right.

GRACE: I'm sorry, I thought…

RUTH: No no no, it's fine.

GRACE: Best to be upfront about these things don't you think?

RUTH: Em…yes I…

TOM: Welcome to *our* house…

RUTH: Well maybe I did have a lot to deal with. I don't know if I can say it was more than anyone else particularly…

GRACE: Well I'd have to disagree…

TOM: Where we're always up front about things…

RUTH: No. Really. All I remember were the questions. Same as you. Why death? Why life?

GRACE: I miss my Mother sometimes but... [you must feel]

TOM: So do I. She's this really nice, polite, sympathetic woman. Great hostess. Did you see where she went? She was here a moment ago, I'm sure she was, sitting on that swing.

GRACE: What was her name?

TOM: Grace.

RUTH: Chan.

GRACE: Chan?

RUTH: Kachanda. Little Sunflower.

GRACE: Beautiful.

TOM: Beautiful.

RUTH: *Tom.* (*A final warning.*)

TOM: What?

GRACE: My mother was called Sarah. Sadie. Loved her statues. Virgins everywhere. In many ways she was worse than my dad.

TOM: He did his best.

GRACE: He adored Tommy of course. Spoilt him rotten.

RUTH: Evidently.

TOM: I didn't leave the trial because I was spoilt.

GRACE: No?

RUTH: You must have been quite a handful, Grace.

GRACE: (*Delighted.*) I was a horrible child. And I knew it too. I operated a split personality. You wouldn't have recognised me. Two wardrobes, two faces, two characters; one for home and one for the world. Home – boring; school projects, school uniform, school everything, more or less what you see today, but back then when I stepped out into the world it was mini-skirts – pussy pelmets we called them, make-up and stilettos and cigarettes. Glamour all the way. Can you imagine? All I really thought about was fashion. Fashion. What happened to me? It all had to be hidden in the shed of course. I used to change in the church.

RUTH: Stilettos in the church.

GRACE: Mm hm.

RUTH: How very radical!

GRACE: Not really, wasn't even in the building, it was always locked. The graveyard.

TOM: You haven't told me this.

GRACE: And I certainly didn't tell your grandfather.

RUTH: Tom said he hit you.

TOM: Ruth.

RUTH: I'm just trying to be up front.

GRACE: Yes. Yes of course you are. Very good. Yes he did hit me. Sometimes. But the real punishment was left to the good Lord, and my guilt. Of which there was always plenty.

TOM: She makes him sound like some perverted old Bible basher. He wasn't.

GRACE: You didn't know him. Anyway, all he ever did was buy you sweeties.

RUTH: Changing in the graveyard. That would have been too scary for me. I slept with the light on until I was nineteen.

GRACE: Did you really? So did Tommy.

RUTH: Did you?

TOM: No.

RUTH: You never told me that.

TOM: Because I didn't.

GRACE: Yes you did.

TOM: Not nineteen!

GRACE: (*Mimicking.*) Not nineteen! Sorry son, am I
    embarrassing you in front of your girlfriend? Sincere
    apologies. Where were we?

RUTH: The graveyard.

GRACE: Yes. Beautifully kept. Lots of flowers. They employed
    a gardener. A nice man. Extremely smelly. Mr Kennedy.
    He used to piss on the geraniums. We liked to spy on him,
    see his willy. Occasionally Mr Kennedy would spot us
    watching and give chase. We got up to all sorts of mischief
    there.

TOM: And Grandpa never knew?

GRACE: If he did he never said anything. But he must have.
    One time I came home, I wasn't very old, fourteen maybe,
    and we'd been drinking cider…

TOM: Cider?!

GRACE: Drinking cider and smoking cigarettes in skirts up to
    our ears. And this particular night, when I was supposed to
    be at some… I don't know, something biblical, I was pissed
    up in the grave yard getting it on with Kevin Johnston. He
    was the local stud. We called him the initiator.

TOM: Wow! No. Too much information.

GRACE: So I was with the initiator, and I must have been
    terribly drunk because I forgot to change back into my
    other clothes. And I came home wearing, you know,
    well, not very much at all really, and I tried to have a
    conversation with him and he hit me too hard *that* night

34

because in the morning my face was swollen, so swollen Tom, that I couldn't go to school, and God the shame! It engulfed the house. He never said a word about it and neither did I. Did you ever do that?

TOM: What?

GRACE: Sneak out and go drinking?

TOM: I just did it in the house.

GRACE: I didn't notice.

TOM: Well you were never there.

GRACE: Do you remember when you came back from America?

TOM: No.

GRACE: Well I do…

TOM: Do you remember when I put the ecstasy into dad's curry? Now that was a classic. I once spiked dad's Chicken Korma with a crushed up E.

RUTH: What?

TOM: Yeah! Mum went absolutely mental and dad was trying to bollock me but he couldn't stop smiling and giggling because he was getting all loved up!

GRACE: That was a bloody dangerous thing to do. Tony didn't know if he was coming or going.

TOM: (*To RUTH.*) It was hilarious though!

GRACE: (*Laughing.*) It was very funny actually.

TOM: Dad loved it. He was trying to score off me for weeks after that.

GRACE: Your father is a fool.

TOM: No he's not.

GRACE: Do you think that's what it was?

TOM: What?

GRACE: That sent you to the Lord. All those drugs.

TOM: No mum. It's a serious thing.

GRACE: Really?

TOM: Yes. (*To RUTH.*) Yes it is.

RUTH: (*Mouthing.*) I know.

> *GRACE notices the conspiracy as TOM smiles at RUTH.*

GRACE: I touched Bowie's sleeve once outside the London
Palladium. Now that was a serious thing.

TOM: What? *David* Bowie?

GRACE: There is only one Bowie.

TOM: Tell his kids that.

RUTH: Well, I'm now slightly less embarrassed about being so
closely associated with your family.

TOM: Oi!

GRACE: How dare you! I am officially extremely cool.
Apparently the junior common room has just voted me the
hippest scientist in College.

TOM: Only because you're a famous atheist. Students always
vote for atheists.

GRACE: Don't…

TOM: Well they do. I did. I definitely did. With my Nietzsche
and my green jeans and my anomie – and the growing
realisation that there is obviously no God out there helping
because once again it's two o'clock in the morning and I
still can't do my essay so bloody hell, I know what'll save
me, I'll vote for a famous atheist whose books I haven't
read yet and that'll sort it all out and validate my human

condition. And you're a woman. An atheist and a women. You're practically vote-rigging.

GRACE: I am not an atheist.

TOM: Okay, okay…whatever.

GRACE: Atheist, young man, is a religious term. Like pro-life. Like intelligent design – you must always define your own terms, I thought you lawyers knew that – the term atheist gives credence to the idea it is pretending to criticise. It's pernicious – a word coined by religions for religions and cleverly snuck into common parlance. Atheist is not a description, it's advertising. I am a naturalist.

RUTH: If you're going to take your clothes off Grace you're going to have to get someone else to swing you.

GRACE: A naturalist as opposed to a supernaturalist.

TOM: I'm going.

GRACE: Don't.

TOM: To find dad.

GRACE: Tom you should listen to this.

TOM: (*Almost gone.*) Yes mum, you're right.

TOM exits. Beat.

GRACE: You don't call someone an afairy-ist or an agoblin-ist, do you now?

RUTH: No Grace, you don't.

GRACE: No. You don't.

Moves fluidly into:

Scene 6

The first anniversary of Tom's death. At Tom's grave. RUTH has brought a little bunch of flowers and TONY has brought a prayer book and a stone to place. TONY takes a hanky out of his pocket and covers his head to say the Kaddish. RUTH stands a respectful distance from him and watches as he reads.

TONY: Yeetgadal v' yeetkadash sh'mey rabbah.

> B'almah dee v'rah kheer'utey
>
> V'yamleekh malkhutei, b'chahyeykhohn, uv' yohmeyghohn,
>
> Uv'chahyei d'chohl beyt yisrael,
>
> Ba'agalah u'veez'man kareev, v'eemru: Amein.
>
> Y'hey sh'met rabbah m'varach l'alam u'l'almey almahyah.
>
> Yeet'barakh, v'yeesh'tabach, v' yeetrohmam, v' yeet'nasei,
>
> V' yeet'hadar, v' yeet'aleh, v' yeet'halal sh'mey d'kudshah b'reekh hoo.
>
> L'eylah meen kohl beerkhatah v'sheeratah,
>
> Toosh'b'chatah v'nechematah, da'ameeran b'al'mah, v'eemru: Amein.
>
> Y'hei shlamah rabbah meen sh'mahyah, v'chahyeem Aleynu v'al kohl yisrael, v'eemru: Amein.
>
> Oseh shalom beem'roh'mahv, hoo ya'aseh shalom,
>
> Aleynu v'al kohl yisrael v'eemru: Amein.

Moves fluidly into:

Scene 7

Before.

TOM: What does dad think about it?

RUTH: Don't open that door.

TOM: No. I want to know. What does dad think about this?

TONY: Dad doesn't give a flying shit.

TOM: What do you mean you don't give a shit.

TONY: *Flying* shit.

TOM: You had me circumcised.

TONY: That was cultural. To save you from embarrassment in the bathroom.

TOM: Embarrassment in the bathroom.

TONY: You would have thought you were weird. You'd have looked at me then looked at yourself and thought you were weird. Deformed. Had a growth. All sons compare themselves to their fathers. They can't help it.

RUTH: I've never been a fan of foreskins, they're pointless and they're ugly.

TONY: (*Pointing finger at RUTH as if to tick her off.*) I am starting to like you more and more.

RUTH: Thank you.

TONY: Welcome to the family.

GRACE: You're completely deluded. Why did I marry you?

TONY: Because you love me. Now is anyone else peckish?

GRACE: Completely and utterly deluded.

TOM: Son's do not always compare themselves to their fathers.

TONY: Yes they do. It's in the brain. Evolution. Ask your mother about it.

GRACE: Actually he's right.

TOM: Son's do not always compare themselves to their fathers.

GRACE: No they do. Not always unfavourably, but they do.

TONY: (*Grinning.*) See!

GRACE: I don't know what you think you have to grin about.

TOM: How could you have let that happen?

GRACE: I didn't let it happen.

RUTH: Don't open that door. That's what I said.

GRACE: Your father did it all by himself while I was at work.

TOM: What, you at work?

GRACE: And do you know what he said to me when I came home?

TONY: (*Delighted, to RUTH.*) I've got a surprise for you.

RUTH: Tony.

GRACE: I've got a surprise for you!

RUTH: You are a truly terrible man.

TONY: Thank you.

GRACE: I have mutilated your child.

TONY: I have saved your child from years of psychological trauma not to mention several potential hygiene issues.

GRACE: He gets it from you.

TONY: How does he get it from me? He doesn't want to be a rabbi does he. Why don't you want to be a rabbi? I can't believe I just asked that. But seriously, why don't you want to be... (*Firmly interrupting himself.*) No. Stop it. Please everyone, ignore me.

TOM: I'm doing the training whatever either of you think.

GRACE: Are you going to say anything to your son?

TONY: A lawyer and a priest. (*To RUTH.*) Are you the book or the sword?

GRACE: Are you going to say anything to your son?

TONY: No. I'm going to get something to eat.

GRACE: Tony!

TONY: It wont matter love. When has anyone ever done anything because of something someone else has said? I'm with Freud on this one. The only thing that motivates people is sex and aggression.

GRACE: You don't know the first thing about Freud.

TONY: I most certainly do.

GRACE: You do not.

TONY: I do.

TOM: You don't dad.

TONY: Yes I do.

TOM: Name one thing you've read.

TONY: Don't be so silly, no one actually reads Freud.

RUTH: I do.

TONY: Now that really is fucked up.

GRACE: You are not becoming a priest.

TOM: I'm not asking your permission Mother, I'm telling you what I'm doing and asking what you think.

GRACE: You're asking for a clip round the ear.

TONY: Just like I said, sex and aggression. All you need to understand.

GRACE: (*Flings something at her husband.*) Shut up! And stay here.

TOM: I should have known better.

RUTH: Yes you should.

GRACE: And what do you think about this?

RUTH: I don't know yet.

GRACE: What do you mean you don't know yet? What about everything you stand for? What about the burden of proof? What about decisions based on evidence?

RUTH: I don't know yet.

GRACE: (*From RUTH to TOM.*) Well I do and I'll tell you exactly what I think.

RUTH: Grace don't.

GRACE: Don't don't me you coward.

TONY: Grace, love.

GRACE: If my son wants to know what I think I'm going to tell him exactly what I think because thought is the precise ingredient most lacking in this ridiculous situation. What I think is, Tom, what I think is that your ignominious toying with faith has always been an extremely irritating adolescent reaction to this family and not just me but also your father but that this, this latest idea of yours, this decision of yours, this…and at your age is… You are too old for this type of teenage revenge. It's ridiculous Tom. It's absurd…

TOM: I know you'll find this hard to believe mum, but my decision is not actually about you.

TONY: (*To RUTH.*) She will find that hard to believe.

TOM: This isn't me just fiddling in my bath. I'm serious about this. There's two thousand years of scholarship and questioning, Two thousand years of inspiration and exploration…

TONY: Five thousand years.

GRACE: What's wrong?

TOM: Nothing's wrong.

GRACE: This is my fault. That summer when you went off to America to build those houses. That was the beginnings of this.

TOM: No.

GRACE: That cunt creationist born again fuck-wit.

TONY: Say it how you see it love.

TOM: He was a lunatic.

GRACE: (*Correcting him.*) He was a lunatic. He gave you all those pamphlets and you were completely seduced. He targeted you Tom. He knew you were my son.

TOM: I thought you would at least be happy for me.

GRACE: How could you have possibly thought that I would be happy for you?

TOM: I don't know.

GRACE: We've given you everything. You have wanted for nothing. Nothing. What is wrong? Something must be wrong.

TOM: Nothing is wrong.

RUTH: I'm pregnant.

Sudden silence. This is clearly news to them all. TOM and GRACE are both stunned. TONY is the first to recover, somewhat in awe of RUTH.

TONY: Well… Right… Well that's… No, that's… Congratulations… (*Laughs.*) Mazeltov! (*Catches himself.*) Congratulations…

RUTH: Thank you Tony…

TONY: No really… Really… I mean it… Congratulations… Honestly, to both of you. Really.

RUTH: Tom.

TOM: Sorry?

RUTH: Tony's…

TONY: From both of us, really…

TOM: (*To RUTH.*) Yeah?

RUTH: Yeah.

> *TOM suddenly grins at RUTH like the Cheshire Cat.*

TONY: Congratulations son. *Congratulations!*

> *And this beautiful moment moves fluidly into:*

Scene 8

Later. GRACE is rehearsing a lecture to herself. Perhaps she is correcting her script. TONY is doing Sudoku.

GRACE: There are four kinds of answer usually given to the question of why religions exist. One: they offer explanations; answers to the basic questions about the origin of the universe, why it exists, what purpose its existence serves, why apparently inexplicable things happen in it and why it includes suffering and death. Two: religions provide comfort, giving hope of life after death and providing reassurance in a hostile world. Also that they offer a way through prayer and sacrifice and good behaviour to get a better deal in this world. Three: religions make for social cohesion; they bind families together…

> *TONY chuckles.*

…consolidate communities and countries, and bring a useful sense of order. And four: religions are born of humankind's natural ignorance and superstitious-ness.

So: Explanation. Comfort. Cohesion. And superstition.

But there is of course a fifth reason offered. A reason which says that there is religion because there is a God...

TONY: Who?

GRACE: Or gods – and belief is simply a response to that fact. This tends to be the religion's own answer.

TONY: Look on the bright side. No one is going to take a priest called Friedman seriously.

GRACE: There are no good excuses for religious belief – not in the West. Not anymore.

TONY: Poverty.

GRACE: What?

TONY: Reactions to global capitalism.

GRACE: Tony.

TONY: He's got a degree in philosophy. What did you expect?

GRACE: A rationalist.

The main point of my talk this evening however, is that more recently we've had detailed psychological explanations for how religious belief works and how it can be understood as a natural by-product of brain function. Two points are important to grasp.

TONY: There are too many numbers in it. Numbers make people nervous.

GRACE: I want to be clear. The first is a point to do with evolution and a phrase I'm sure that you will all recognize: survival of the fittest. For survival, the child's brain has evolved a sponge like ability, absorbing all information that it is given by the adults and the culture that looks after it. In the same way as the child learns language without questioning so it learns not to play near the cliff's edge and so it learns religious belief. Simply to survive it is prudent that the child's brain believes everything that it is told and this is why, for example, ninety-eight per cent of children who are brought up by Muslim parents become Muslim.

The second point about how our brains work helps us to understand why we so easily believe in ghosts and gods. This is a feature of how our minds organise concepts. Our minds can detach concepts from their ordinary uses while keeping most of their standard inferential connections, and then join them to other concepts to form strange and even contradictory new combinations. And this is how we generate notions of the supernatural. For example: our earliest ancestors heard thunder and saw lightning, so they imagined that there were invisible giants walking about on the clouds with mighty footsteps. They took an ordinary concept (the concept of a human being) with its standard inferential connections (human beings walk about) – and then joined it to the idea of something huge, like a mountain, but invisible, like the wind – and out of this amalgam they made a god – a god causing thunder in the sky by stamping on the storm-clouds.

What do you think about it?

TONY: It's good. And you're right the numbers do help.

GRACE: No. About Tom.

TONY: Oh…yes, you know, well, I was surprised but I have to say I'm genuinely very happy for him. I am. I mean I think it was a bit of a shock, but he'll be a great dad and she's smashing…

GRACE: No Tony. This priest crap?

TONY: Oh.

GRACE: I just can't understand.

TONY: Know then thyself presume not God to scan;
    The proper study of mankind is man.

GRACE: Damn right. Who is that?

TONY: The Pope.

GRACE: The Pope? Which Pope?

TONY: There is only one Pope – Alexander Pope!

GRACE: Answer my question.

TONY: Em, well, you know, Tom's always been a Romantic.

GRACE: So have you.

TONY: But he's cleverer than me and he's had way too much education so I can see why he likes Christianity over Judaism, I mean…the holy trinity and all that…takes some mental gymnastics that God in three parts stuff – I suppose it's sufficiently complicated for him and I don't know, he seems happy, can't you hate the sin and love the sinner?

GRACE: I feel like a failure.

TONY: Oh love, don't.

GRACE: Don't tell me what to feel Tony.

TONY: Then don't tell Tom what to believe. If anyone tried telling you what to think you'd hate it. And it doesn't matter that you're right, it doesn't matter at all, it's not the point, he's finding his own way, exploring and questioning and he's trying to involve us, which is a damn sight more that either of us did with our parents, so give him a bit of respect for that at least. He's going to do what he wants with or without us, so come on, 'sweet moderation, heart of this nation'.

Enter TOM.

TOM: 'Desert us not, we are between the wars.' Billy Bragg.

TONY: Great man.

GRACE: But are you disagreeing with me?

TONY: No I'm not, I'm just adding a bit of popular culture to the proceedings.

GRACE: Because I don't think you understand how important this is to me.

TONY: I really do.

TOM: What's this?

GRACE: With what we are capable of...

TONY: One guess.

TOM: Ah.

GRACE: The violence we are capable of...

TONY: Did you know that the Dalai Lama fixes watches?

GRACE: What?

TONY: I thought you could use it in the blind watchmaker bit. He's mad on small gadgets apparently. Loves repairing them.

TOM: Really?

TONY: Apparently.

GRACE: Where do you get this stuff from?

TONY: No idea.

GRACE: So what are we going to do?

TONY: About what?

GRACE: (*Pointing at her son.*) Him!

TONY: Nothing. Be nice.

GRACE: Be nice?

TONY: Yes.

GRACE: Be *nice*?

TONY: Because he's our son.

GRACE: I thought we'd watched the news together Tony. Didn't we? Are either of you living in the same world as I am?

TONY: Don't open that door.

GRACE: (*Exasperated by TONY's reply. To TOM. Very direct.*) You bear a heavy responsibility in all of this.

TOM: How?

GRACE: Because your lot provide cover for these nutters.

TONY: You'll regret this Grace.

GRACE: (*To TONY.*) Be nice! (*Back to TOM.*) It's the heart of the issue. The basic problem. Because you and your religious moderation just don't permit anything critical to be said about religious extremism. Religious moderates – if there really can be such a thing which I very much doubt when push comes to divine shove – religious moderates, bare a huge responsibility for encouraging religious violence, because their language and beliefs…

TOM: My language and beliefs.

TONY leaves them to it.

GRACE: Yes. (*To TONY.*) Coward! (*Back to TOM.*) Yes! Because your language and your beliefs provide the context in which scriptural literalism and religious violence can never be adequately opposed.

TOM: Yeah.

GRACE: What do you mean yeah?

TOM: I mean yeah. It's a problem. It haunts me. Do I provide cover for these nutters?

GRACE: Yes.

TOM: For the fanatics.

GRACE: Yes.

TOM: Yes! Am I defending a whole y'know, which actually has about it all sorts of things I loathe. I hate the violent...but I think that the dangerous...the dangerous situation to get into is to see the world as a battle between those that have religion and those that don't. Where those that have religion are defined as zealous, whereas for me it's actually...there's a really important role for those that want to say we need to have *better* religion.

GRACE: That's selfish Tom.

TOM: No it's not. It's not selfish.

GRACE: It's the excuse that allows you to hold on to this leap of faith you make. But if you can glimpse, as you say you can, even for a moment, that you might, even possibly provide cover for these people then it's a price too high.

TOM: Reasonable doubt.

GRACE: Oh come on!

TOM: What I'm trying to do is to help people to feel that it's fine to be thinking, self-critical, left-wing and religious. And they are not the most dangerous people in the world mum, they're not the ones to lose sleep over. If I provide cover I provide cover for that lot. I don't provide cover for sexist, homophobic, bigoted people who put bombs on planes. I did that when I was a lawyer. Now all I ever do is attack them. My world view is closer to yours than it is to theirs. But life is complicated. And even the most ardent atheist has to...

GRACE: I am not an atheist.

TOM: You know what I mean, fine, even the most ardent naturalist, has to admit that life is complicated. It's not straightforward. I am an enlightenment person and I'm religious.

GRACE: That's a contradiction in terms.

TOM: Exactly. And I live with that. That's what I am.

GRACE: No. You can't have it both ways. Not today. Not in our context. It doesn't work, you have to choose.

TOM: It's not a matter of which side I'm on.

GRACE: Grow up. Yes it is.

TOM: Contradictions are what people are, bundles of contradictions, fighting them and working them out. And I wont be dictated to by your overly simplistic logic-chopping approach to life.

GRACE: I beg your pardon?

TOM: You always want to limit experience to the cold theoretical but I'm telling you – the truth has to be sieved in lots of different ways.

GRACE: No. No it doesn't – I can't believe what I'm hearing – it's exactly that kind of slippery talk that needs attacking. Talk that allows religion to demand being treated reasonably. Because it shouldn't be. Because religion is not reasonable. It's instinctively fundamentalist because it believes it is right without feeling the need to provide reliable evidence? Come on you haven't forgotten everything you used to think. At best, it's nonsensical, ridiculous but religion is rarely at its best and at its worst… we saw it again today, just turn on the television. Read a paper. Listen to the radio. Tom. Son. Wake up. Rigorous rationale, proportioning belief to evidence, is not me being cold simplistic, logic-chopping. It's being sensible, careful, considerate. Being sceptical and critical and insisting on evidence is uncomfortable and difficult and boring but it is the one thing we can truly rely on because it is a belief system that allows itself to be proven wrong.

TOM: (*Very facetious.*) So let's take religion out of society.

GRACE: (*Responding to his tone.*) Tom.

TOM: And while you're about it let's take away sex.

GRACE: Son.

TOM: Dad's right about that, sex and aggression, it's what most of the fights are about on Saturday night. Let's get rid of it. Let's do test-tubes.

GRACE: I am not modeling a fascist state where everyone walks around in white suits and smiles!

TOM: I don't live in your world. I live in the real world where religion is present everywhere.

GRACE: And that's precisely the problem. Because the ultimate basis of religious morality is divine command, whatever up-dated gloss you put on it. And it's too dangerous because there are so many different divines commanding. Morality has to be about recognising and respecting and tolerating people for their own sakes, no divine sanction required.

TOM: I'm not trying to pretend that it's not dangerous sometimes. I think that's absolutely the case. I just think – I suppose – one of the things to do in terms of a strategy and I'm being realistic and pragmatic here, okay, because we have to ask ourselves, what sort of strategy for dealing with these nutters are we going to adopt? Do we want an all out culture war between your pure enlightenment thinking and bad religion or is there a value, is there, let me put it another way, is the answer to bad religion – practically – no religion or better religion? Who is more likely to defeat bad religion? Good religion or atheism? Now that's a question. A real question. So stop attacking me mum because I'm your hope. Because you are never going to turn the world's religious into atheists. If that's what your battle is. If that's what you are trying to do, you're going to lose. And so are we all. The best you can hope for is to turn bad violent religion into better religion and that's what I'm trying to do. So no, I'm not providing cover for the nutters. By wasting your time attacking me it's you're absurd purism which is letting them off the hook because you're never going to win that battle.

GRACE: We've made too many concessions to religious belief. It is one of the most pernicious sources of conflict in our world and you, my son, are one of its salesmen.

TOM: And you're the fundamentalist mum.

GRACE: Fuck you.

Beat. TOM exits.

Tom. Tom?

TONY enters.

TONY: Only me.

GRACE: Sorry. I thought…

TONY: No.

GRACE: I couldn't stop myself Tony.

TONY: Neither could he by the sound of it.

GRACE: Why couldn't I stop myself?

TONY: Because it's important.

GRACE: (*As if correcting.*) Yes it is.

TONY hugs her.

TONY: It'll be alright.

GRACE: Will it?

TONY: We'll all go out for a curry. Take some ecstasy.

GRACE: D'you remember that?

TONY: Every time I hear music with a drum beat.

TONY does his dance move. GRACE laughs.

GRACE: I know what I should have said. It was when I was a student and we had this professor, ancient man, Dr John R Baker. And for as long as anyone could remember he had taught that the Golgi Apparatus…

TONY: The what?

GRACE: The Golgi Apparatus. It's a feature of the interior of cells.

TONY: What does it do?

GRACE: It doesn't matter.

TONY: Right.

GRACE: No, sorry love, but it's not important, the point is that Dr Baker taught that this thing wasn't real. For years he'd argued the same thing: The Golgi Apparatus is not real, it's an artefact, an illusion. Anyway. One Monday afternoon the whole department's gathered to listen to some visiting researcher – it was the same every week – but this Monday the visitor was an American cell biologist. And to our growing shock and embarrassment we began to realise that this researcher was presenting completely convincing evidence that the Golgi Apparatus was real. It wasn't an artefact after all. It was a very dramatic moment for the zoology department. The whole room was avoiding making eye contact with Dr Baker. It was awful. And do you know what he did at the end of the lecture? At the end of the lecture the old man stood up and strode to the front of the hall, grabbed the American by the hand and with tears in his eyes said, 'My dear fellow, I wish to thank you, I have been wrong these fifteen years.' We were all stunned. Stunned. I felt very very ashamed because of what I guess I'd thought my own reaction would have been had I been in his shoes. I clapped my hands red. I remember it like it was yesterday. Now that's a serious response to the world. A response on which I can place my moral compass. I should have told Tom that.

TONY: My dear fellow, I wish to thank you, I have been wrong these fifteen years. Nice. Classy.

GRACE: No religious person could ever say that.

Moves fluidly into:

Scene 9

Later.

TOM: Brian.

RUTH: Edward.

TOM: Derek.

RUTH: John.

TOM: Norman

RUTH: Robert.

TOM: That was Grandpa's name.

RUTH: Sorry.

TOM: Doesn't matter. Kevin.

RUTH: Kevin. Definitely. Anything pop star-ish.

TOM: Yup. Anything politiciany.

RUTH: Richard, Ted or Dick.

TOM: Goes without saying. Pubert.

RUTH: Pubert?

TOM: Pubert.

RUTH: (*Okay then.*) Archibald.

TOM: Fester.

RUTH: Elvis.

TOM: Lurch.

RUTH: *The Addams Family*!

TOM: *The Addams Family.* If it's a girl.

RUTH: Maureen.

TOM: Sharon.

RUTH: Tandy.

TOM: Olive.

RUTH: Olive's not a name.

TOM: Yes it is. Someone I know has an aunt called Olive.

RUTH: Really?

TOM: Yup.

RUTH: Okay. Olive or anything vegetably.

TOM: Or anything flowery. Lilly, Poppy, Bluebell…

RUTH: Rose.

TOM: I like Rose.

RUTH: Too late buster, you binned her.

TOM: An Olive isn't a vegetable you know.

RUTH: I know. And nothing herby.

TOM: Herby!

RUTH: No. Like Sage or something.

TOM: Oh.

RUTH: Or Saffron.

TOM: Oh yeah. Definitely. What about Chan?

    Beat.

RUTH: Oh. I never thought of that. How weird.

TOM: Kachanda. Beautiful.

RUTH: It is flowery though.

TOM: Special dispensation. I really like it.

RUTH: I really like you.

TOM: Yeah?

RUTH: Yeah. (*They kiss.*) Mostly. (*Beat.*) Tom I'm finding all this priest...you know...

TOM: Yeah?

RUTH: Yeah, a bit.

TOM: Me too. Guess where dad took me?

RUTH: Bengal Tiger.

TOM: Yeah.

RUTH: No E-s this time I hope.

TOM: No. And we started talking and I told him I was going to ask you to marry me.

Beat.

RUTH: What?

TOM: Yeah.

RUTH: Tom?

TOM: Yeah. And he said to me are you sure you're doing the right thing?

RUTH: What?

TOM: Yeah.

RUTH: It's a little late for that isn't it? (*Indicating pregnancy.*)

TOM: That's what I said.

RUTH: That's your bloody Mother that is.

TOM: No it's not. He said it's what fathers are supposed to do.

RUTH: It's your Mother.

TOM: But it was good because it helped me understand something, how to explain and... Look...so we'd had a couple of beers and I tell dad what I'm planning and he says are you sure you're doing the right thing? So, then he says, grab the napkin, so I grab the napkin and he says down the middle, draw a line down the middle and put all the sort of pluses and all the minuses for why this is a good thing. And so I drew all this and I tried to write down all the pluses…so y'know, she's cute and stuff…

RUTH: She's cute!

TOM: And stuff.

RUTH: Tom!

TOM: Lots of stuff.

RUTH: Have you still got this napkin?

TOM: Stop it. Listen to me. So you do the whole list of things and then you suddenly realize, or I did at least, I realized that that list could never add up to what I was about to do. However poetic or intelligent or clever or in touch with my own emotions I was, the sum total of that list on the plus side could never equal: I love this person – and want to marry them for ever.

RUTH: Tom…

TOM: Look – I need to explain this to you. That there comes a point when my justifications run out but I know that being a priest is just what I have to do. Just like I do about marrying you. I just know. And that's the area where my faith is located and it's not on the list.

RUTH: Is this a proposal Tom because if it is I mean, do you really expect me to say yes?

TOM: I'm serious.

RUTH: So am I.

TOM: I know you're finding this difficult and you are being brilliant to me but I really need you to understand, and the nearest analogy to it, I think I can find is love. Love. So you're going to give away your whole life, you commit

your life to this one person on the basis of this feeling.
And what is it, this y'know, this when your talking about
this other umm…you could produce an expert to say, to
reduce love to some sort of chemical imbalance in the
brain or to some sort of sociological need or whatever it
is, you could do that so as to undermine, I would say well,
thank you, thank you very much but actually I'm still not
interested, this love is more real to me than however true
those explanations are, so there is something not on the
list, something that exceeds the list, your grasp about it
and that's where I give myself over to that y'know, I give
myself over to that and do you see? Is it better to be in love
or not in love? I dunno. I'm in love. And it's not on the list.

RUTH: Because I don't believe in God Tom. And I really don't.
And maybe I won't mind church – sometimes – because
I like the rituals. But I don't believe and I don't want you
to try and persuade me or our children. Is that going to be
too difficult for you?

TOM: I'm not sure I believe in God, that God exists. I'm really
not sure existence is the right word. The closer I get to it
the less it seems to be there. But it just won't go away.

RUTH: Is that going to be too difficult for you?

TOM: I know you're finding all this priest crap… And to tell
you the truth, most of the time I don't want it to be there. I
don't. I don't want to think about it, I wish it wasn't there,
I wish I could get on with my life, go back to the law and
make some money and make you happy but it just keeps
on coming back and just haunts me as this thing I should
be doing. Almost despite myself it's, y'know, I can't make
complete sense of it, but I think… Oh God I'm going to
sound like a wanker, but it feels like a *calling*…the fact that
it won't leave me alone. It's stuck there like a bloody great
big rock that I can't ignore… People think religion makes
people happy. But it doesn't. It doesn't make me happy. I
think the thing that makes most people happy in the world,
and this is my theory…

TONY suddenly enters. GRACE follows.

TONY: No, this is my theory!

TOM: Dancing!

TONY: Dancing! (*Now rave music. TONY starts dancing as if on ecstasy.*) Dancing is what really makes people happy. It's got everything, its got human contact, its got other people, its got sex, its got a bit of movement, its got everything, physical, y'know, dancing is it, and yeah I think pretty much – dancing is what makes people happy.

TOM is now dancing as well and he grabs RUTH who joins in. GRACE doesn't dance.

Oi! What's this? (*TONY moves his arms and legs as if he is a jellyfish.*) God moving in a mysterious way! Ha!

RUTH: The day after you first stayed over at mine. Do you remember?

TOM: Course. I wooed you with my move. (*Does the move.*)

RUTH: The next day I called Laura and told her I thought you were a really good dancer!

TOM: Little did you know.

RUTH: One move Friedman.

TOM: Thank you. (*He does his move.*)

RUTH: And then we spent that first Christmas with your parents and I realized who you'd stolen it from.

TONY: One move Friedman. (*Does the move.*)

GRACE: Tony sit down.

RUTH: I like your dad.

TONY: You're not alone.

GRACE: Tony. You'll have a heart attack.

TONY: Right.

TONY sits down beside GRACE.

TOM: It's like in the… (*He can't remember the name of the film so does some crap Kung Fu moves as a prompt.*)

RUTH: *The Matrix.*

TOM: *The Matrix*! The first one, the others are rubbish, you fell asleep I think but the first *Matrix* is a great film.

RUTH: I didn't fall asleep. I took you to see that film.

TOM: Are you sure?

RUTH: Tom.

TOM: Really? It's very self-consciously religious, y'know…

RUTH: I know.

TOM: Trinity and so forth…

RUTH: You're unbelievable.

TOM: And Keanu Reeves gets born again and stuff, but…but there's a line in it where what's his name…

RUTH: Neo.

TOM: Yeah Neo, Neo's sitting there with – who's the black guy? – just before he takes this pill…

RUTH: Morpheus.

TOM: Morpheus…and he says something like um… I can remember exactly the line, he says, 'You've had it, haven't you, a splinter in the mind,' he says, 'you have a splinter in the mind.' 'This splinter in the mind that you've never known quite what to do with, you've never quite known what it is, and its this thing that you just cant…' 'And the splinter in the mind is the…' something, this is not quite it, y'know, and you take the red pill and you get to see it, or you get the blue pill and you go back to how you were.

So do you take the red pill or the blue pill. And that's what I've got, a splinter in the mind, that just wont go away. I sound crazy.

RUTH: Bonkers.

TOM: I love you. And I know you love me.

RUTH: I'm reconsidering.

TOM: Marry me.

RUTH: Is it going to be too difficult for you that I don't believe in God Tom?

Moving fluidly between TOM's *reality and* GRACE's *reality which is now the day after* TOM's *death.*

GRACE: And what did he say?

TOM: (*A new thought.*) Is it going to be too difficult for you that I do?

RUTH: (*To* GRACE.) He didn't reply.

TOM: Marry me.

TONY: And what did you say?

TOM: Marry me Ruth.

RUTH: He didn't ask.

TONY: Oh.

TOM: *Ruth!*

TONY: Oh, I'm so sorry love.

TOM: Marry me.

RUTH: Yeah.

TONY: Shit.

RUTH: Yeah.

TONY: Shit. But do you know…what he would have wanted?

TOM: Hold on. (*Goes to find a book; Philip Larkin's complete works.*)

RUTH: Yeah.

GRACE: He means for the funeral.

RUTH: I know.

GRACE: You do?

TOM: I find it very difficult to put into my own words.

RUTH: He wanted a mass.

GRACE: A mass.

RUTH: He thought it was beautiful. The ritual. The sharing of bread and wine.

TONY: (*Understanding.*) Right.

GRACE: No.

TONY: (*Agreeing.*) Right.

RUTH: That's what he wanted.

TOM: Here we go. Page ninety-seven. This is what I'm trying to say.

GRACE: No way.

TOM: It's beautiful.

GRACE: It's terrible. We can't.

TONY: No. Right.

GRACE: I mean we just can't. How can we? A mass?

RUTH: That's what he wanted.

TOM: Once I am sure there's nothing going on
I step inside, letting the door thud shut.
Another church:

GRACE: A mass. Well we can't. A small private service is enough…

RUTH: Enough? Would Tom think it was enough?

GRACE: Ruth. The people who did this, they…

RUTH: Tom wasn't killed because of what he believed Grace.

GRACE: Ruth. Think. Be reasonable.

RUTH: How? *How?*

GRACE: It's wrong. We can't.

TOM: And he goes through what he does in this church and he looks around and em and…

…Mounting the lectern, I peruse a few
Hectoring large-scale verses, and pronounce
'Here endeth' much more loudly than I'd meant.

RUTH: My dad was an atheist. I buried him. Organised his funeral. He was, I don't know, he hated religion. And at the funeral we didn't say a word because it wasn't right. Because he would have hated it. So we said nothing. And it wasn't enough. It really wasn't. Not nearly. (*Goes to find an identical book to the one TOM is reading from.*) And I don't pretend to share what Tom believed but at the service… There's something I'd like you to read Tony. If you think you can. You probably know it. I'd do it but I don't think I'd manage… It's Larkin. And it's the end of… it's in here somewhere…

GRACE: Ruth we can't.

RUTH: I'm going to bury Tom the way he wanted.

GRACE: No.

RUTH: We have to.

GRACE: I won't have it.

TONY: Grace, love.

GRACE: Tony help me. Please.

RUTH: We have to.

TONY: Look we're all…

GRACE: No!

RUTH: Yes!

TONY: (*Absolute and absolutely out of character.*) Stop! Both of
you. Just absolutely stop.

TOM: And stop I did: in fact I often do,
And always end much at a loss like this,
Wondering what to look for; wondering, too,
When churches fall completely out of use
What we shall turn them into…

RUTH: (*Searching the book.*) It's called 'Churchgoing', it's a
poem called 'Churchgoing' which is about Larkin going
into a church, page ninety-seven. He talks about what will
happen…

TOM: Then he talks about what will happen in the future…

RUTH: In the future…

RUTH starts to cry but controls herself by finding the place.

TOM: Where he says superstition, like belief, must die and I
think that's probably wrong, and I think that Larkin does
too because of what he says at the end…

RUTH: From here.

TONY: A serious house on serious earth it is…

RUTH: That's it.

TOM: And this is what I'm trying to say.

TONY: A serious house on serious earth it is,
In whose blent air all our compulsions meet,
Are recognised, and robed as destinies.

And that much never can be obsolete,
Since someone will forever be surprising
A hunger in himself to be more serious,
And gravitating with it to this ground,
Which, he once heard, was proper to grow wise in,
If only that so many dead lie round.

GRACE: We can't do this Ruth.

RUTH: We have to.

GRACE: No.

RUTH: If you deny Tom the funeral he wanted, I swear to
Christ Grace, you will not be part of your grandchild's life.

The crackle of a loudspeaker.

Did you hear what I said?

MICHAEL: Is this working? Can you hear me, professor?

Sound of feedback.

GRACE: Sorry?

RUTH: Because I promise you…

GRACE: Yes. I heard you.

MICHAEL: We can hear you, professor. Is everything all right?

Moves fluidly into.

Scene 10

Later. GRACE is giving a lecture. She wears a gown. Her usual resolve is even stronger.

GRACE: It is true that I don't speak passionately about Norse
Gods. This is because nobody believes in them anymore.
But I probably would if I lived with people who believed
in them and were killing each other in the name of Thor

and Wotan. But belief in Jesus is rife in the world and belief in Allah is rife in the world and people like my son have died because of it.

The United States of America is run now by born again Christians, by people who act because they think their prayers are being answered. In America, in a presidential election, an actor who reads the Bible would almost certainly defeat a rocket scientist who does not. And that country is our World's Policeman. And who are they currently in charge of policing? Islamism. Islamism is not the moderate self-critical belief system that my son preached for. Islamism is a credal wave that calls for our own elimination. The most extreme Islamists want to kill everyone on earth except the most extreme Islamists.

Now religion has always been extremely sensitive ground. And at this point because I am going to talk about Islam and Islamism, and for my own safety, I need to make it clear that I respect the prophet Muhammad. I respect him as an historical being. I need to make it clear that it is not an individual that I seek to criticise but a religious belief system. A belief system which can be so sensitive to what it can define as insult, and so violent in its revenges, that for my own safety, I need to make this statement.

Moves fluidly into:

Scene 11

The Bengal Tiger. TONY has taken TOM for a curry. They are just starting their second pint of beer. TONY munches on a poppadom.

TOM: I just don't think about it like that, so I prefer to put it in a different sort of way. I suppose I want to see different religions as different languages. I speak Christianity and with the language I speak, there are certain things I can show and certain things I can reveal which can't be revealed in other languages. Eskimos have fifty words for snow. They can see a whole lot of things that, y'know, there's a truth opened up by the language that I speak about God which I don't think can be exposed in other languages. So what I'm saying is, that is, I do think Christianity's the best. However what I don't want to say is that Christianity is…the fact that I affirm Christianity is that I necessarily think that the others are not true. It's like saying, speaking English…we don't have to affirm our Englishness by denying French or Urdu. What do I want to deny other languages for? I want to see religions as languages for talking about the divine. And if you see them as languages, Christianity doesn't contradict Islam just as English doesn't contradict French.

TONY: But Christianity does contradict Islam doesn't it? I mean Islam says Jesus was a minor prophet and Christianity says that he was the son of God. That sounds like a big difference to me.

TOM: I don't mean it like that. I'm not a literalist. I'm saying that the two religions are separate and equally valid approaches to dealing with the divine.

TONY: The sigh of the oppressed creature, the heart of a heartless world, the soul of soulless conditions.

TOM: The opium of the people.

TONY: Great man.

TOM: It's mum's language I'm having trouble with.

TONY: Right.

TOM: It's why I'm always stuffed in conversations with her – Every point has a number, everything must be clear. All problems answered by a league table. It's radical empiricism! I mean, do you really want to live in a world like that? I don't.

TONY: (*Sighing.*) Oh dear…

TOM: Why do you love her so much?

TONY: Bloody good question.

TOM: I'm serious.

TONY: So am I.

TOM: Dad.

TONY: Fear.

TOM: Dad.

TONY: Really. A great aphrodisiac fear.

TOM: I'm serious.

TONY: Admiration I think.

TOM: What?

TONY: Yeah. I've always admired your mother. It's true she has an unfortunate manner, but y'know, I've always thought she was right about stuff.

TOM: Really? Right.

TONY: Yeah. Yeah. And her commitment to what she believes, what she wants for the world. Her hopes. You know. You becoming a priest is genuinely very difficult for her.

TOM: I know. I've let her down.

TONY: No don't. Of course you haven't…

TOM: And I couldn't stop myself.

TONY: Yeah. Well. It's important to you.

TOM: (*As a correction.*) Yes it is.

TONY: It'll be okay.

TOM: Will it?

TONY: We'll all go out for a curry. Take some ecstasy.

TOM: D'you remember that?

TONY: Every time I hear music with a drum beat. You don't have any do you?

TOM: What?

TONY: E.

TOM: No!

TONY: I'm only asking.

TOM: Dad! I'm going to be a priest for fuck's sake!

TONY: Yeah. A priest.

TOM: A priest.

TONY: A priest...called *Friedman!!*

Father and son laugh.

Oy vey! Maria!

TOM: Why did you never...you know...?

TONY: Me?

TOM: Yeah.

TONY: Don't know really. It just never made much sense to me. And you know I'm just an old lefty at heart. I approve of the values, some of them, the compassion, but on the whole I see more evidence for its lack and I don't really approve of the structure and...you know, I'm too petty and schoolboy to resist the wind-up. The only religion I really enjoy is Hinduism and that's purely because it annoys religious Jews so much because it's just so much older than anything else. They hate that. And I love it that they hate it. Sad but true. Keeps me going. And there's other things too like the Hindu stories are more colourful and it's got no founder, thank God, and there are lots of Gods to choose from and it kind of admits it's a messy indefinable thing and of course I couldn't do it because apart from anything I'd miss the beef. But don't get me wrong, all that's positive and bollocks, I like it best because it pisses off the Orthodox. And Christianity is tricky for me, and I am very proud of you and all that, and I don't think you're turning on the gas or anything, I mean I hope you know that, and I can see it makes you happy and that's more or less good enough for me, but Christianity you know... Tricky. Even for a non-practicing lefty, and not just because of the historical example it has set in its relation to power, I mean, barbaric, but you know all that and it's fine now and everything because the church has no teeth and that's exactly the way it should be if you ask me, but it's because of sin and punishment and is it really very humane to believe in everlasting punishment and I don't know but, and I'm sorry for being all Jewish all of a sudden but it's because at some point it, y'know all this son, Christianity does become personal to Jews because eventually it's the Jews who get the blame for bungling the initial you know, the thingy.

TOM: The Crucifixion?

TONY: Yeah. Exactly. So there you go. That's me. Tony Friedman on religion. I'm starving where's our food?

TOM: I'd just like mum to...understand.

TONY: She might not son.

TOM: I know...

TONY: Just give her some time to get used to the idea.

TOM: Yeah.

TONY: Did you know that Muhammad's ninth wife was a Jew?

TOM: No.

TONY: Yeah apparently. Saffiya. Her father fought against Muhammad's armies, lost and Muhammad took a shine to her. Saffiya. Means pure and enlightened. When Muhammad was challenged by his followers for marrying an infidel he said, she is a righteous woman, she comes from the people of the book, we have no quarrel with the people of the book. (*Laughs: As if!!*) *We have no quarrel with the people of the book!!* I was thinking it was a nice name for a girl.

TOM: How do you spell it?

TONY: S-a-f-f-i-y-a I think.

TOM: It's a bit too like Saffron.

TONY: Saffron?

TOM: The herb.

TONY: Saffron's not a herb, it's a spice.

TONY: Is it?

TONY: Yeah. I like Ruth. I really do. She scares me a little. Smashing girl.

TOM: Yeah?

TONY: Yeah. Smashing. How is she?

TOM: She loves being pregnant.

TONY: Your mother was the same. Bloody hell. Women. How do they survive their bodies?

TOM: I'm going to ask her to marry me.

TONY: Good.

TOM: You think?

TONY: Absolutely. Though if your mother was here she'd want me to make sure you're doing the right thing.

TOM: It's a bit late for that isn't it.

TONY: Yeah but no harm in thinking. Grab that napkin.

Moves fluidly into:

Scene 12

TOM's funeral.

RUTH: I'm going to read something by Tom's favourite poet. Philip Larkin. It reminds me of Tom, because he used to recite it to me and…and it's for Tony and especially for Grace who should take full responsibility for today's *private* service.

> They fuck you up, your mum and dad,
> They may not mean to, but they do.
> They fill you with the faults they had,
> And add some extra, just for you.
> But they were fucked up in their turn
> By fools in old-style hats and coats,
> Who half the time were soppy-stern,
> And half at one another's throats.
> Man hands on misery to man.
> It deepens like a coastal shelf.
> Get out as early as you can,
> And don't have any kids yourself.

Moves fluidly into:

Scene 13

Some months later. GRACE takes some pills.

GRACE: Well he wanted me to have a religious experience.

TONY: Just don't take too many.

GRACE: (*Snaps out of all proportion.*) Please don't tell me what to do Tony!

Beat. Recovers but not fully.

Are you going to leave me?

73

TONY: No.

GRACE: It's just I thought you might need to. Because of…

TONY: No.

GRACE: …of how I've been behaving.

TONY: Yeah.

> *Beat.*

GRACE: If I were you I'd…

TONY: You're not me.

GRACE: Perhaps you should think about it.

TONY: Don't tell me what to do Grace.

GRACE: No. Sorry.

> *They look at each other.*

I couldn't let…

TONY: I know…

GRACE: Tom's funeral. I couldn't let…

TONY: I'm not sure we were right about that.

GRACE: Tony. I keep seeing him everywhere.

TONY: Call Ruth.

GRACE: I can't.

TONY: Call Ruth and say sorry.

GRACE: I can't.

TONY: What was it the guy said?

GRACE: Who?

TONY: The Goldi Apparatus man.

GRACE: Golgi.

TONY: Golgi. What did he say? My dear fellow, I wish to thank you, I have been wrong these fifteen years. You clapped your hands red.

GRACE: (*This is why she loves him.*) How come you remember that?

TONY: Don't know. It's an inspiring story. Call Ruth.

GRACE looks at her husband.

Moves fluidly into:

Scene 14

TOM at seminary, giving a sermon.

TOM: For most religions the other is the god. But I think that we've got to stop thinking about God as a proper name, for a *thing*, as if the word God refers to some sort of object in the universe. Because that's just bollocks. Complete and utter bollocks. And in fact, I think it's quite easy to demonstrate through traditional Christian theology that God is not a *thing* at all. If you trawled the world y'know, if you made a manifest of all the things in the universe including tables and chairs and glasses and wine, there would not be on that list a thing called God. God cannot be the creator of everything and something on the list of things being created. This is not some new-fangled theology, by the way. Aquinas said all this centuries ago. God's not a thing, y'know it's not as if once you've added up all these, the furniture of the universe, you go, 'oh yes and plus one more thing'. No. God doesn't exist on that manifest of things that exist in the universe. God's just not like that. To that extent the atheists are right: There is no such thing as God. And actually…and I think that is there straightforwardly in the Bible…which is… I mean the great story of what God is like in the Bible, it seems to me is the story of the Golden Calf and Moses going up the mountain. So you get the mountain, you got Moses going up the mountain – *this is the great story of religion I think* – Moses travels up the mountain. The higher he gets up the mountain, it gets cloudier and cloudier and cloudier, so the nearer to God, the nearer to this other he gets less and less able to see less able to know his way about, okay, down below, okay, what's happening down below is all of them are making God into this thing, a Golden Calf and they're trying to make, y'know, it's like they're trying to make God into this physical thing. So you've got this contrast, by the journey to the real divine which involves lostness, y'know, doubt, not being able to see, not being able to grasp this, this this, this y'know, this notion of God, no-thinglyness. And yet, at the bottom of the mountain there's this sort of real *thing* and they all bow down to it. But it's a con. And the whole story is saying that God isn't like any thing we expect. That's why it pisses me off when the atheists keep on trying to tell me what sort of God I believe in. It pisses me off that they assume what I believe. Because they want me to believe in a thing called God. But I don't. I don't believe God is a thing. I just believe in God.

Moves fluidly into:

Scene 15

Ani DiFranco's 'Untouchable Face' from her live album 'Living in Clip'. RUTH comes to the front of the stage and is spot-lit. In her imagination she becomes DiFranco giving her concert. During the track TONY enters wearing a dressing gown and slippers. He's woken up again in the middle of the night and comes downstairs to sit for a while. RUTH and TONY do not acknowledge one another. Later, and to coincide with the last verse of the song, GRACE comes to stand beside RUTH. RUTH sings some of the last verse to GRACE. During the above, autumn leaves fall followed by snow then blossom then green leaves then autumn leaves again. And this journey through the seasons ends as the song is made to suddenly stop, at TOM's grave

RUTH: Sometimes I just need to use other people's words

GRACE: Has Tony done this?

RUTH: Last year. He didn't sing, he said a prayer. In Hebrew. It was beautiful.

RUTH takes two cups, a large bottle of cider and some cigarettes from her bag.

Cider and cigarettes. To make you feel at home.

GRACE: Thank you.

RUTH: To… What was his name?

GRACE: Who?

RUTH: The initiator.

GRACE: Kevin Johnston

RUTH: To Kevin Johnston.

GRACE: To Kevin.

They toast and drink.

Though to tell you the truth, he didn't actually initiate me. He tried his best but no cigar.

RUTH: Cigarette?

GRACE: No thanks.

RUTH: (*Lighting a cigarette.*) I initiated Tom.

GRACE: Sorry?

RUTH: In a rowing boat.

GRACE: Gosh.

RUTH: Though initiation is a very generous way of putting it. I seem to remember it started off very well but… I only went out with him again out of pity.

Beat.

77

GRACE: I think I will have one of those actually.

Passes her a cigarette.

RUTH: It was at the beginning of my final term. I knew he liked me so I let him take me rowing.

GRACE: I feel embarrassed Ruth.

RUTH looks at her: 'Good'.

RUTH: Nowhere near as embarrassed as he did. He was a very proud boy, his mother's son after all.

GRACE: I'm sorry.

RUTH: (*Like a bullet.*) You really fucking should be. Two years Grace. You're a fucking idiot.

A moment.

GRACE: I… (*She has nothing to say in her defence.*)

A moment.

RUTH: With you and Tom it was always the same, it was always about love. Love, love, love. You loved your work. He loved his God. You loved your son. He loved his mother. God how he wanted your approval. He couldn't keep away, it was almost pathetic. And Tony. Poor Tony, he looks so sad now. Lost his sense of humour but – and how you love Tony is so weird – but I know how much he loves you. And that's why I loved Tom and his fucked up family because of all that passionate love whooshing around. And I did love it, love you all, even you who were so fucking rude all the time, I even loved you… But y'know, I'm less sure about love these days, less sure that it's the most important thing because it's just too much sometimes. Just too unmanageable. Don't you find, unmanageable to the point of, *I* do, because it so easily becomes and it does become, it really does, it becomes ferocious. I see it every day. I even see it in court. Cornered animals. Wounded and wilful and what for, I

think love mostly. Love. And what is it? I mean *you* could
tell me Grace, couldn't you, of course you could, you could
describe it, use the correct language, delineate and separate
and explain, explain this thing, this feeling. This feeling
that we can't do anything much about except inflict on
other people. Or try not to but that's very difficult. Seems
to be. That's the problem. And I do understand, I get it. I
do, I get it. I look at little Chan and she's so helpless and
she's mine and my responsibility and I get it over and over
and over. Overwhelmed. Overwhelmed. And I choke on
it. Every day. And that's why I think it's wrong, completely
wrong to give love such status, such celebrity when it's just
so unbelievably dangerous, I would kill for that child. Kill.
Not a problem. No hesitation. For her I would destroy.
Absolutely. Mutilate someone. Like Tom was mutilated.
You know. And I think. I'm coming to think, *believe* in fact
that it is kindness Grace – kindness, that's the big one, not
love. That's what I'm coming to believe Grace, and it's
probably the more boring – definitely – kindness – because
it's calm and considerate and hesitant and certainly the
more difficult one to do. I find anyway. I really do. And I
might not have had much love at home but I had that and
I didn't even notice. Fuck! It didn't even occur until… My
mum. Remember, you said Tom told you. Do you? Well I
didn't understand… (*To the sky.*) And I'm sorry mum that
I didn't but I do now and I think you were actually trying
to be kind mum and I'm… Before she killed herself she
typed out letters for me and dad and she couldn't type so
it must have taken her a long time and a lot of planning
so she must have given her suicide a great deal of thought
and wanted to leave everything just so, in a certain way,
she re-did her will, cleared out her cupboards and get this,
she threw away her perfumes. Her perfumes. All of them.
Threw them away. You know, so we wouldn't have to smell
her. (*To the sky.*) And mum I didn't understand but I think
you were actually trying to be kind… And I'm p… I am
mum, I'm p…

RUTH stops.

But I'm not you see. Am I Grace? I'm just not... Fucking hell. Every year I try. Every year and now with... Fifteen years mum. Fifteen fucking years. And I can't say it mum because I don't mean it. Because I'm not *proud* of you! Not at all! I don't even want to understand you! Because I'm still untrusting and closed and angry, always angry because of you, because you were a coward mum and you didn't want to understand me! And you killed dad and you fucked me mum, you totally fucked me and look at what's happened! I go off in search of extremes like a fucking magnet. Ha! And I found it. I did. I found it. I found it in college, I found it at work and most of all I found it with her son. And I don't want to smell you any more mum, I want to smell him. *Him.* And he's not here. And you wanted to leave everything neat and tidy and I didn't understand until they blew my life up...and what happened to all those people. And Tom just because he was there. Just because he was there. Just because he was there. What am I going to do? What the fuck am I... And when I started to love him and let him love me I thought I'd found what I thought had been missing... and I lost him but this time with such a mess. Such a ferocious mess... And I thought about you mum and how tidy you had been. And still... Still.

I was baptised when I was nineteen. Never told Tom. Didn't last. And the thing is...that I think about is Tom... And I've waited until now to say it...waited for my chief witness to arrive because she was right about one thing Tom, she was right about me being a coward. Because... because I'm not sure I was going to be able to marry you. Really. I'm not sure I was going to be able to – He did ask me, of course he asked and I lied to you – because, because you didn't deserve the truth – because...because I suspect, and this is the truth Tom, I suspect you were going to love your God more than you were going to love me and... (*Shakes her head.*) And I've been thinking about that tortured man twisted on his cross and I understand the inspiration but, you know, I need to be the most important thing. I need that. Because of everything and... But we have a beautiful baby. We absolutely do. And she has your eyes and I'm okay when I look at them, most of the time...and I miss you...and I tell her about you or I try to, and your dad does his dance move when he's singing her to sleep, and the Queen of Hearts is still down here swinging away with her axe and she has never seen her granddaughter because... Because...

RUTH looks at GRACE then sits down, pours herself another drink, drinks it and then pours another. They drink. Eventually:

GRACE: I see him everywhere.

RUTH: Do you?

GRACE: Yes.

RUTH: I don't. Just in Chan.

Beat.

GRACE: When Tom was born I understood something about life. That I wasn't at the centre of it anymore. It was a shock. Well, you know. You know exactly the strength of that feeling. And of course you could kill for that feeling. Tony always said so. The transfer of the centre of interest from ones self to another. On the one hand most unsettling, on the other, quite a relief. And having Tom...

RUTH: You should tell him.

GRACE: What?

RUTH: You should tell him.

GRACE: It's not really my style.

RUTH: (*Hard.*) Yeah? So how's you're style been working for you Grace? Good is it?

Beat.

GRACE: Having Tom...

81

RUTH: You.

GRACE: What?

RUTH: You. Having you…

GRACE: Don't bully me Ruth. I'm here.

RUTH: Try. And with having you…

GRACE: …life seemed to make more sense somehow.

RUTH: And with having you…

GRACE: Please…

RUTH: And with having you…

GRACE: (*Dominating.*) Life seemed to make more sense and the I was, my 'I' which was firmly at the centre of me and which I had loathed, really, loathed, well it moved, it moved, and he was the cause, Tom, he moved it, he did. And I wasn't there enough. And I didn't tell him. But I was there really, because I thought it was important, fundamental not to be there each time he needed me because we have to know, we have to, that we're on our own – we're on our own – there's no cosmic purpose – no plan – just being, just being and that's it, and I didn't know that, I wasn't taught that, you see, wasn't shown how to be on my own and it…

RUTH: Don't talk to me Grace until you're finished with your son because one thing is certain you are not finished with him and you need to start being.

Beat. To begin with almost unemotional.

GRACE: And all this faith. These codes to please invisible fathers. These promises of heavens and hells to come. God. Well it's absurd. All of it. All of it. It's absurd and dangerous and it's wrong. And someone else to blame, I mean… Just look at life. It is so unlikely. So gloriously unlikely but not because of anything. It just is. It just is because… because… An over simplistic logic-chopping approach to life, Tom called it. He couldn't feel satisfied with the rational outlook. Wanted to turn violent religion into better religion. Better religion. (*GRACE looks at the sky and smiles.*) And somewhere inside me, so help me, some *disgusting splinter* inside of me thinks, and so help me this is true, thinks that you Tom, you stupid fucking…fucking earnest, beautiful boy of mine, that in some way you got what you deserved. (*A crack beginning.*) You got what you deserved. You got the poem you were looking for. I'm sorry but I keep thinking it, I know it's not true but it's why I'm being cruel to everyone who shows me anything but pain because I don't want pity I want scorn. I want *scorn.* I want *scorn.*

Only now do GRACE's suppressed emotions crack through her and into the world. For a time GRACE is out of control. RUTH watches her, then comforts her. Time passes. As GRACE recovers…

RUTH: Who are you talking to you mad woman.

GRACE: (*Laughs.*)

RUTH: Have you gone crazy, this is a fucking church.

GRACE: I'm sorry about…

RUTH: Yeah right. Blow your nose, you're as bad as your granddaughter.

RUTH gives GRACE a hanky. GRACE blows her nose

GRACE: A serious place for serious people.

RUTH: I dunno. I'm more with the gardener. Piss on the daisies.

GRACE: Geraniums.

RUTH: Geraniums. That was it. I'm going to light a candle.

GRACE nods.

You want to come? Even atheists need to light the occasional candle.

GRACE shakes her head.

GRACE: I'm just going to sit here for a while.

RUTH: Sure?

GRACE: Yeah.

RUTH: Okay. See you in a bit.

RUTH goes. Beat.

Moves fluidly into:

Scene 16

TOM enters and sits beside his mum. Some time passes before…

GRACE: I've been invited to Canada.

TOM: Canada?

GRACE: Yeah. There's a neurologist out there trying to give people religious experiences?

TOM: In Canada?

GRACE: Mmm.

TOM: In Canada? That sounds a bit suspicious if you ask me.

GRACE: You're as bad as your father. But Tony said I should go. Thinks it'll do me good. He makes it sound like a Pilgrimage.

TOM: It could be.

Beat. GRACE looks at her son.

GRACE: I doubt it.

GRACE smooths TOM's hair with her hand.

TOM: How is he?

GRACE: He's sad son. He's really sad. He misses you terribly and tries to hide it for my sake. And I've been no help. Working. Lecturing. Horrible. You can imagine.

TOM: Yeah.

GRACE: What do you mean yeah?

TOM: I mean yeah, I can imagine.

GRACE: Mmm.

TOM: How do they give it to you? The religious experience.

GRACE: (*Chuckles.*) You wear this sort of motorcycle helmet...

TOM: Motorcycle helmet?

GRACE: Mm, it holds the electrodes in the correct position.

TOM: Electrodes?

GRACE: (*Laughs.*) And they tape ping-pong balls over your eyes.

TOM: Ping-pong balls...

TOM exits. GRACE does not seem to notice.

GRACE: To help with concentration apparently.

TOM:

GRACE: (*A joke.*) They call it the God Helmet.

TOM:

A speaker crackles.

GRACE: You don't see anything, it's more like feeling something, a presence.

MICHAEL: Like a ghost?

GRACE: No. Not really. I mean as far as I can gather you stimulated the right hemisphere of my brain and then the left.

MICHAEL: Yeah.

GRACE: The region we best think controls the idea of self followed by the area which controls language, which then interprets the stimulation as a sort of sensed entity.

MICHAEL: Exactly.

GRACE: So I felt that.

Another crackle as TONY and RUTH enter. Now it is the present.

TONY: And this man actually gets paid to do this?

GRACE: It's important work…

TONY: Right.

GRACE: Michael Persinger thinks it's this stimulation and misinterpretation that's responsible for almost anything we describe as paranormal: aliens, heavenly apparitions, dead relatives. The implications are huge.

RUTH: I see dead people. What's that from? That film with thingy in it.

TONY: Don't know.

RUTH: Oh come on you do, that's going to drive me mad now.

TONY: Well I for one prefer life to have a little more mystery. And I refuse to let anyone reduce my sense of the spiritual to brain static. Especially a Canadian.

GRACE: I told you already, he's not a Canadian, he's an American.

TONY: Well what's he doing in Canada then?

GRACE: It's just where he works.

TONY: Come off it. No one just works in Canada. It all sounds highly suspicious if you ask me.

GRACE: Well no one did dear.

TONY: The God Helmet. Talk about leading the witness.

RUTH: So who did you see?

Silence. Although TOM is no longer on stage his presence is felt by them all. Silence.

TONY: Sense.

RUTH: Sorry, sense. *The Sixth Sense*!

TONY: What?

RUTH: The name of the film.

TONY is not TOM.

Sorry. Who did you sense Grace?

TONY: Did you...sense anyone?

A speaker crackles.

GRACE: No. I... (*A new resolve, mostly for TONY's sake.*) No. It didn't really work on me. I just sort of felt floaty and remembered something Ruth had told me about her and Tom in a rowing boat.

TONY: A rowing boat?

RUTH: Grace!

GRACE: Yes?

TONY: What's this?

RUTH: Nothing. I can't believe you...

TONY: A rowing boat? Doesn't sound like nothing to me.

The speaker is now a baby monitor and CHAN can be heard crying.

RUTH: Oh here we go again.

TONY: Saved by the baby.

GRACE: I'll go.

TONY: No, stay where you are and talk behind my back. A rowing boat.

GRACE: No I mean I'd like to. (*Beat.*) If that's okay?

RUTH: Yeah. Of course it is. Thank you.

GRACE exits. TONY looks at RUTH and smiles. He obviously has something on his mind.

Are you okay?

TONY: Sometimes. You?

RUTH: Sometimes.

TONY: Thanks for coming.

RUTH: It's nice to see Grace.

TONY: Yeah. Em… Look… I found something the other day and I didn't know if I should just throw it away but in the end I didn't and em, well, here. (*TONY hands RUTH a napkin with a line down the middle and some writing on it.*)

RUTH: What is it? (*RUTH reads the napkin and realises what it is.*) 'She's cute.' Oh Tony…

A moment. Then through the speaker we hear:

GRACE: Hello there, and what's wrong with you? Yes. Yes. What's wrong with you? Come here and give Grandma a big hug, that's right, and then she'll tell you all about the Blind Watchmaker. Yes, you like the sound of that don't you. Blind Watchmaker!

TONY and RUTH look at each other: GRACE is unbelievable! Beat. Then we hear GRACE through the baby monitor. A clear change of tone, speaking now to her eavesdroppers.

Bloody got you both didn't I! Blind Watchmaker! I got you! Ha! I know I got you. (*To CHAN.*) I know I got them…

TONY: (*Getting up. Lying.*) She didn't get me.

RUTH: (*Also lying.*) Me neither.

TONY: I'm starving. Do you want something to eat?

RUTH: Yeah. I'll come with you.

TONY: Come on.

TONY and RUTH exit.

GRACE: I got you... Yes, Grandma got them didn't she, yes she did, Grandma got them cause Grandma's very clever isn't she, yes... And just look at your beautiful eyes, just look... (*Suddenly struck.*) Gosh. (*Beat.*) Exactly like your dad. Yes. That's right love. Exactly like your dad...

Several beats. Lights down slowly.

The End.